Mitchell Symons was born in London and educated at Mill Hill School and the LSE, where he studied law. Since leaving BBC TV, where he was a researcher and then a director, he has worked as a writer, broadcaster and journalist. He was a principal writer of early editions of the board game Trivial Pursuit and has devised many television formats. He is also the author of more than thirty books, and currently writes a weekly column for the Sunday Express. *Why Eating Bogeys Is Good For You* won the Blue Peter Best Book with Facts Award in 2010 and he repeated this success with *Do Igloos Have Loos?* in 2011.

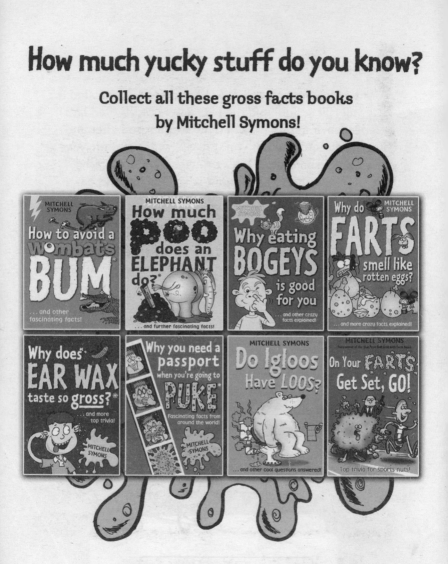

Don't wipe your BUM with A HEDGEHOG

Mitchell Symons

RED FOX

DON'T WIPE YOUR BUM WITH A HEDGEHOG
A RED FOX BOOK 978 1 849 41191 2

First published in Great Britain by Doubleday,
an imprint of Random House Children's Publishers UK
A Random House Group Company

Doubleday edition published 2012
Red Fox edition published 2012

3 5 7 9 10 8 6 4

The Random House Group Limited supports The Forest Stewardship
Council® (FSC®), the leading international forest-certification organisation.
Our books carrying the FSC label are printed on FSC®-certified paper.
FSC is the only forest-certification scheme supported by the leading
environmental organisations, including Greenpeace. Our
paper procurement policy can be found at
www.randomhouse.co.uk/environment

Set in Optima

Red Fox Books are published by Random House Children's Publishers UK,
61–63 Uxbridge Road, London W5 5SA

www.randomhousechildrens.co.uk

Addresses for companies within The Random House Group Limited can be
found at: www.randomhouse.co.uk/offices.htm

THE RANDOM HOUSE GROUP Limited Reg. No. 954009

A CIP catalogue record for this book is available from the British Library.

Printed and bound in Great Britain by Clays Ltd, St Ives plc

**To my sons Jack and Charlie:
with love and thanks.**

INTRODUCTION

I have previously published eight trivia books. This time around, I've decided to do something a little different. The background to this book is a 'question' I posed in *Why Do Farts Smell Like Rotten Eggs?*: YOU'RE AN OLD MAN, MITCH, SO WHAT'S YOUR BEST ADVICE?

And here are a few things that I wrote:

Never eat yellow snow.

Talk slowly but think quickly.

Never wipe your bum with a hedgehog.

Never laugh at your own jokes.

When you're asked how you are, say 'I'm well,' NOT 'I'm good.'

Never walk up the down escalator.

Never shop in a store that won't let you use its toilet.

Don't take chocolates from the lower layer until you've finished all the ones on the top layer.

Respect the personal space of large growling animals.

Don't be embarrassed by bodily functions.

Never say 'in my humble opinion'.

Never visit a funfair with a full stomach.

Never wear a baseball cap back-to-front unless you want to shrink your IQ.

Never swallow the water in a public swimming pool.

Never look down on anyone unless you're helping them up.

Never forget it's easier to stay out of trouble than to get out of trouble.

Never try to teach a pig to sing. It wastes your time and annoys the pig.

Never have a staring match with an owl.

Never tie your shoelaces in a revolving door.

Never argue with an idiot. Bystanders can't tell the difference.

Never, ever make absolute, unconditional statements.

If you and your friend are being chased by a mad dog, don't worry about out-running the mad dog, just worry about out-running your friend.

Never play leapfrog with a unicorn.

As you can see, it was merely an excuse for me to list some of the funnier pieces of advice I'd collected over the years. Having said that, there were some serious things in there, and so when I was deciding what to write next, it got me thinking: What if I did a WHOLE book of advice – a mixture of funny and serious and, above all, true?

I've had a wealth of experience – good and bad – and I have two sons (both now adults) who are fine, decent men, so if I'm not qualified to offer advice, then who is?

Ultimately, though, YOU'LL be the judge of whether I've got it right.

And that turns out to be my very first tip of the book: *Make up your own mind.*

Now for some important acknowledgements, because without these people, this book couldn't have been written at all:

(in alphabetical order) my editor Lauren Buckland, my wife and chief researcher

Penny Chorlton, my publisher Annie Eaton, and the designers Dominica Clements and Nigel Baines.

In addition, I'd also like to thank the following people for their help, contributions and/or support: Gilly Adams, Luigi Bonomi, Paul Donnelley, Jonathan Fingerhut, Jenny Garrison, Bryn Musson, Nicholas Ridge, Mari Roberts, Jerry Sawyer, Charlie Symons, Jack Symons, Louise Symons, David Thomas, Martin Townsend, Clair Woodward, Rob Woolley and Tom Woolley.

If I've missed anyone out, then please know that – as with any mistakes in the book – it is, as I always say, entirely down to my own stupidity.

Mitchell Symons

www.mitchellsymons.co.uk

LESSONS TO LIVE BY

Never spit on a rollercoaster.

Remember: there are three kinds of people. Those who can count and those who can't.

Always be sincere – even if you don't mean it.

89 per cent of statistics are made up. The other 63 per cent are wrong.

If all else fails, eat chocolate.

Be naughty – save Santa the trip!

Don't arm-wrestle yourself.

If you can't say it in 50 characters, then don't b

Never trust a person who says 'Trust me . . .'

Never pee uphill or into the wind.

GENERAL ADVICE

Don't care too much what others think of you.
The fact is, they don't think about you that much as they're too busy worrying what other people are thinking of them!

Don't just 'know' things – any fool can do that – the point is to *understand* them.
Knowledge – in itself – is useless (except in quizzes) unless you learn how to use it. However (says the quiz king), NEVER underestimate the importance of quizzes!

Step outside your comfort zone from time to time.
It'll help you see life from a different angle and make you appreciate your comfort zone all the more!

Embrace simplicity.
Simple is best! Avoid making things any harder than they need to be. Which is why

I'm known by my friends as Simple Symons (not that I ever met a pieman going to the fair).

Never mistake activity for action.

The two aren't necessarily the same. In fact, very often activity – frenzied, unstructured activity – can actually get in the way of positive, meaningful action. This also gives you the excuse to sit back and do nothing while your friends are charging about all over the place!

Be nice to nerds. Chances are you'll end up working for one.

At school, the rough, tough, sporty types rarely amount to much, but the quiet geeky child whom no one talks to (except to tease) might very well end up rich and successful. Worth cultivating now . . . And if you yourself are the nerd, then I know you'll be thanking me right now!

Be eccentric now.
Don't wait till you're older. Just think how much fun you could be having making people wonder what on earth you're doing!

Don't congratulate yourself too much or beat yourself up too much.
Somewhere in between is probably about right.

Don't let yesterday take up too much of today.
Yes, we can all learn from the past, but if we spent too long holding inquests into what's gone on before, we'd be permanently living in the past – and if you kept on doing that there'd be no present and so (if you follow my rather daft reasoning) no past for the future! I know what I mean!

Don't blame the computer.
Computers do what you tell them to do – not what you want them to do.

Don't just learn the tricks of the trade; learn the trade.
Any fool – the author is just such a fool – can pick up the odd fact that makes them sound like an expert on a subject; the thing is, however, to actually master that subject.

Don't tell me how hard you work; tell me how much you get done.
It's all about what you produce; not the effort that goes into it. If you achieve the same success as someone else with half the sweat, then that's your business. Similarly, don't tell me how long something took you and expect me to be more impressed with the result. One hour's brilliant revision is worth eight hours of preparing colour-coded revision timetables!

Put yourself in other people's shoes.
If something would please or hurt you, then it would almost certainly please or hurt the other person too. Don't take me too literally and start asking your friends to take off their shoes so you can put them on . . .

Don't give up.
*You can keep going long after you think
you can't. Doesn't just apply to runs and
long walks. In fact, probably doesn't apply
to them at all . . .*

**Avoid making important decisions when
you're extremely tired or hungry.**
*And that advice even extends to not even
SAYING anything too important when
you're obviously not in the right frame of
mind and might regret it later. I avoid this
particular pitfall by sleeping and eating far
too much. Well, it's one solution!*

Don't hate Mondays.
*You're going to spend 1/7th of your life
there.*

**Never eat spaghetti with anyone you're
hoping to impress.**
*On the other hand, if they can tolerate
you eating spaghetti, then they'll probably
forgive you anything! (Well, That's My
Experience Anyway!)*

Don't use a big word where a smaller one would do.

There are people who use language to try to impress (or intimidate) people. Having said that, never be scared to use a 'big word' if it happens to be the appropriate word for the occasion. So that's another supercalifragilisticexpialidocious piece of advice!

Don't compare yourself to the best that others can do, but to the best that *you* can do.

There's no harm in having an idea of how good other people are at lessons or at sport, but you only have the power to do YOUR best – not THEIR best.

Remember the compliments you receive, forget the insults.

I know it's impossible – if I receive 99 compliments and just a single insult, the insult will prey on my mind for days – but I'm not telling you to do what I do but just to do what I say! With that in mind, please

now go straight to online book sites and give this book a five-star review!

Never agree to 'something a little different this time' at the hairdresser's.
Apart from anything else, you'll have to put up with comments from your friends along the lines of 'It'll grow on you.'

Don't be the last to laugh at yourself.
Sometimes we say or do things that are unintentionally funny. The sooner you see the joke, the sooner it's over – and you'll have had a laugh and proved yourself to be

a good sport into the bargain! I've learned to laugh at myself – not because I'm funny but because I'm always doing stupid things. And at MY age . . .

Take a lesson from crayons.
They're all different colours, but they all have to live in the same box. Yup, I've been raiding Christmas crackers for advice.

Never say a funny thing to a person who doesn't have a sense of humour.
Applies doubly to scary teachers.

Don't be the one your parents warned you about.
You know what I'm talking about . . . yes, YOU!

Don't lose your self-control.

*Applies equally to genuine emergencies
(where you must keep your head) and
hissy fits (where there's really no need to
throw your dummy out of the pram). There
has to be control. If you lose self-control,
then someone else will take over and you
won't like it.*

Don't get too obsessed with any hobby.

*There is a very fine line between 'hobby'
and 'obsession'. Especially applies to
computer games.*

When you have nothing to say, say nothing.
Don't fear silence and don't talk for the sake of it. Remember, you don't have to explain something you never said, and a closed mouth gathers no foot.[1]

It's good to be original, but beyond being original is just being an idiot.
Very often the coolest person we know is also the most original (and vice-versa), but there's nothing less cool than the person who tries too hard.

Don't feel guilty if you don't know what you want to do when you're older.
Older people ask you that question because they don't know what else to ask you. Assuming you don't know, just say 'I don't know.' Alternatively, try asking them the same question . . .

---

1   Editor's note: Isn't it about time you followed your own advice, Mitch?

Learn to trust people.

Even if that trust is occasionally misplaced, it's still better than going through life not trusting people. Once again, almost certainly doesn't apply to brothers and sisters . . .

Remember your mum's birthday but forget her age.

Much better than the other way round.

Do the right thing – if only to surprise people.
That shouldn't be your motivation: you should do the right thing for the right reasons, but it is also fun to surprise – or even shock – people!

Always talk to people as if you were being watched by someone you wanted to impress.
Or whatever it takes to get you to be nice to people!

And while we're on the subject, never tell someone that 'shouting never solved anything' when they're, er, shouting.
It'll only make them even angrier!

Never follow the crowd.
At least, not because you want to keep in with the crowd. Also because it'll become too crowded.

When someone asks you to move the piano, don't offer to move the stool.
If you genuinely want to help, then you

have to do what the other person wants you to do and not what you can be bothered to do.

Don't say you don't have enough time.
You have exactly the same number of hours a day as all the great scientists, artists and explorers had. Just make sure you use that time wisely. Though to be fair to you, all the great scientists, etc., never had the distractions of the Wii and stuff like that!

Avoid people who pay compliments like they expect receipts.
And don't do it yourself! Compliments should be genuine, and no one should be keeping score. Unless, of course, you happen to be winning . . .

Never start a sentence with 'basically'.
Basically, because it's annoying . . . Oops!

Be happy for your friends when things go well for them.
Anyone can sympathize with the sufferings of a friend, but it requires a really good person to be supportive of a friend's success. And you'll like yourself so much more as a result!

Buy a bird feeder and hang it somewhere you can see it.
Feeding the birds – especially in winter – is a kindness that brings its own reward in the sight of grateful birds eating.

Read like you can't get enough learning.
It's a sad fact that children tend to read

more than adults do, so make the most of
these years and take every opportunity to
read. I take a paperback with me wherever
I go, so I always know that I've got
something to occupy my time. And it's SO
much more rewarding than fiddling with
a mobile phone! Especially when, like me,
you've got podgy fingers!

Find a poem you like and memorize it.
Yes, I know it'll feel a bit like a party piece,
but there's nothing wrong with having a
party piece. Especially at parties.

Be well-mannered.

People – especially grown-ups – will forgive an awful lot if you're polite and courteous. Just think how much you could get away with if you were polite at the same time!

Win without boasting; lose without excuses.

Above all, be gracious in both victory and defeat so that someone looking at you wouldn't know whether you'd won or lost. Obviously doesn't apply to cricket matches between England and Australia . . .

Relax.

Except for rare life-and-death matters, nothing is as important as it first seems. This advice is not an excuse for you to avoid doing homework . . .

Spend less time worrying *who's* right, and more time deciding *what's* right.
Well, which do YOU think is more important?

When you don't know what you're doing, at least do it neatly.
To mess up AND to leave a mess is just wrong!

Never queue at a ticket office behind someone with a rucksack.
They almost certainly won't know what it is they want or where they want to go.

Learn to listen.
Opportunity sometimes knocks very softly.

Be cheerful even if you don't feel cheerful.
It'll make others cheerful, and before you know it, you'll be feeling cheerful too!

Admit your mistakes.
No one thinks any the worse of you for making a mistake, but they might if you deny it or try to make feeble excuses for it. And by the way, don't make the same mistake twice.

Return things you borrow.
And make sure that they're in the same – or better – condition than they were before. And that applies double to things borrowed from elder brothers or sisters . . .

Let people know what you'll stand for – and what you won't.
Another way of saying that you should let people – especially new friends – know what your limits are. My limits are two Big Macs and a large portion of fries . . .

Never expect anyone to do anything you wouldn't do yourself.
If you're reluctant, haven't they got the right to be too? And saying 'I dare you' doesn't make it any more right!

Become a person who brightens a room just by entering it.
What a lovely ambition! And one I'm still waiting to achieve . . .

Don't trust a man/woman who doesn't like dogs.
Well, I don't trust people like that!

Be modest.
*I'm talking about genuine – not false –
modesty. Most of us have got a lot to be
modest about, and remember, an awful
lot was accomplished before we were
born. My friends tell me I have more to be
modest about than most people . . .*

Memo to self: MUST change friends.

Never be too busy to meet someone new.
*It's important to get out of your comfort
zone. Who knows – that new person might
one day turn out to be your best friend!*

Never put off apologizing.
*If you're going to apologize – and it's
almost always a good idea to do so – then
do it immediately and graciously.*

Never hurry a good time.
*Make the most of it: take the opportunity
to enjoy yourself rather than rushing on to
the next experience. Particularly applies to
funfair rides.*

Say nice things about people.
You'll never regret it. Also, try this as a rule of thumb: be nicer behind someone's back than you are to their face.

When you're not having a good day, help create one for others.
It might even turn your own day around!

Don't talk unless you can improve the silence.
There's nothing wrong with silence, you know. Sometimes the best kind of friend is the kind you can sit down with, never say a word, and then walk away feeling like it was the greatest conversation you've ever had. This DOESN'T apply to me as I'm NEVER silent . . .

Never try to tell everyone everything you know.
It may take too short a time!

If you find yourself in a hole, stop digging.
In other words, if you've accidentally

insulted someone, don't try to explain what you meant to say; just apologize and leave it at that.

Don't automatically assume that anyone stepping out of a stretch limo is a celebrity.
In fact, they almost certainly aren't!

Never mistake personality for character.
It's what people are like underneath that counts.

Read the directions, even if you don't follow them.
At least know which 'rules' you're breaking. It also helps if you don't throw away the instructions with the packaging . . .

Don't laugh just because everyone else is laughing if you don't find it funny.
You might be in a theatre or a cinema, or even just playing with a group of friends, but if you don't find something funny, then don't laugh just to be 'in the gang'.

Never bother to read anything supposedly written by a celebrity.
Allow me to let you in on a secret: most celebrities – not all, but most, and

especially footballers – are better at what they do for a living than they are at writing about it. That's why ghost writers – people who write books or articles for them – were invented. So when your friends are rushing out to buy a book with a celebrity's name on the cover, bear in mind that not only have they probably not written it, they very likely haven't even READ it.

Always avoid people who describe themselves as 'crazy!!!' or 'mad!!!'
They're just extremely annoying!

Don't believe everything you think.
*I have to stop myself from doing this.
Sometimes you find yourself saying things
that sort of sound right, but when you stop
to think about them you realize that you're
wrong.*

Never miss a good chance to shut up.
*Generally speaking, you aren't learning
much when your mouth is moving.*

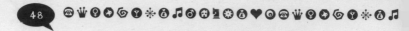
If you're given an opportunity, take it.
In other words, seize the day or you'll regret it. Never forget, opportunities always look bigger going than coming.

When you give a lesson in meanness to an animal or a person, don't be surprised if they learn their lesson.
They'll almost certainly turn round and bite you . . . and so will the animal! This is very similar to the following piece of advice:

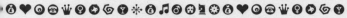

When you're throwing your weight around, be ready to have it thrown around by somebody else.

I never throw my weight around – not because I'm a nice guy but because I'm fat . . .

Don't beat yourself up because other children are better at a subject than you are.

Truth is, everybody is ignorant . . . only in different subjects. Believe me, there is – or there will be – something that you're really good at!

Never offer to teach a fish to swim.

In other words, if someone knows more about something than you do, don't

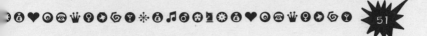

lecture them about it. The trick, however, is to know that the person is more knowledgeable than you are BEFORE you open your mouth . . .

Speak properly.
It's important to pronounce the whole word and not just the first few letters. Also there are two 't's in 'butter': please feel free to use both of them.

Read more books[2] and watch less TV.
I'm not knocking television – I LOVE television . . . so much so that I sometimes have to tear myself away from it to read books. The difference between the two is that TV gives you instant entertainment while books offer you a deeper satisfaction.

Sing in the shower.
And not just in the shower! It's (almost) impossible to be unhappy if you're singing. Doesn't apply first thing in the morning when your parents are asleep . . .

---

2   And I don't mean just my books!

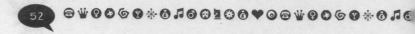

Never miss an opportunity to use the toilet.
When a parent or a teacher offers you an opportunity to go to the loo, then do so,

because if you don't, you can be sure that you'll need to very soon afterwards.

Never judge a book by its movie.
Just because you liked the film doesn't mean you'll like the book on which it was based. And vice-versa.

Don't obey all the rules or you'll miss all the fun.
The trick is to know which rules can – occasionally – be broken and which can't.[3]

Be the person everyone wants to sit next to.
That's if you aren't already!

Never tell a teacher (or, later in life, a boss) that you have nothing to do.
For as sure as night follows day, they will find something for you to do . . . and it almost certainly WON'T be something you want to do!

Accept that some days you're the pigeon, and some days you're the statue.
Sometimes you're the windscreen,

3　　Note to parents and teachers: the author takes no responsibility for rules broken . . .

*sometimes you're the insect. In other words, some days are 'your' days, when everything goes right . . . and some days aren't.
Just accept it.*

If you can't be kind, at least be vague.
'Yeah, that's, er, really, um, good, you know.' Especially applies when your mum asks you if she looks nice in an awful new dress . . .

Don't wait.
The time will never be just right.

Give everything you've got.
Pain is nothing compared to what it feels like to fail or to give up.

Never own problems that should belong to the person who gave them to you.

I used to live in a suburb of West London, where I had a neighbour who used to (illegally) reserve a car space in our road. Whenever he took his car out, he'd leave some planks of wood – what we came to call 'the contraption' – in its place.

I tried reasoning with him, but he insisted that because the space was in front of his house, he was morally entitled to it.

But what about other residents' guests? If we all did what he did, there'd never be anywhere for them to park. Didn't his guests park outside our houses?

Yes, he said, they did, but that was our fault for not putting out 'contraptions' ourselves.

So, in other words, he was taking advantage of our goodwill.

This became a source of annoyance to me, and one day I mentioned it to my father, who'd come over for lunch.

'It's about the ownership of a problem. This really ought to be his problem, but he's given it to you so you're going to have to return it to him.'

'But how?' I asked him.

'It's easy,' said my father.

And so it was.

Within five minutes we'd dismantled the contraption and chucked it in a skip.

'Now it's his problem,' said Dad.

My elder son was just ten when I first explained the matter of 'ownership of the problem' to him.

He'd come home from school and told me about a couple of older lads who'd been bullying him.

I immediately phoned the school head teacher and told her.

Then I said to my son, 'Look, Jack, those two boys gave you a problem, right? You *gave it to me. I gave it to Mrs Sinclair, and tomorrow she'll give it straight back to the boys. Who's going to own that problem?'*

'Them,' he said. 'The boys.'

'And who deserves to own the problem?'

'Them, Dad.'

'That's right, son. Sleep well.'

Don't get mad – get even.

Pick battles big enough to matter, small enough to win.

Even if you're right, there are only so many fights you can pick. After a certain number, you're just marked down as someone who loves fighting.

Never attribute to nastiness what can easily be explained by stupidity.

Judging by you and me, most people are more likely to be stupid than nasty, so let's try to give them the benefit of the doubt, eh?

Always be wary of people who boast about their high IQs.

The problem isn't the high IQ – it's the boasting. I myself have a very high IQ, but I hate to boast about it . . . Oops!

Don't idolize rich people just because of their wealth.

After all, a rich person is nothing but a poor person with money (think about it!). And don't assume that wealthy people will be more generous to you. In fact, the opposite is more likely to be the case: that's why they're rich . . .

Money is a lousy way of keeping score.

For a start, you probably shouldn't even be keeping score, but if you have to, money is a silly place to start – or to finish. How much money a person – or their parents – has/have is no indication of how successful/decent/ fulfilled they are. If you really must keep score, then judge a person by their friends – and not by the quantity but by the quality of those friends. Even then, it's silly, isn't it?

Make the most of your life.
In particular, remember the lovely line that life may not be the party we hoped for, but while we're here we should dance. Even if, like me, you can't dance . . .

Don't be afraid of your doubts.

More people should have doubts. The whole problem with the world is that fools and fanatics are always so certain of themselves, but wiser people are so full of doubts. I'm always doubting myself – so does that mean I'm wise? I hope so!

Beware of people who are chatty in the morning – especially during breakfast.

Oscar Wilde said, 'Only dull people are brilliant at breakfast,' and he was right.

Don't assume that other people are happier than you just because they look happier.

There's a story – and it's almost certainly just that – about a sad man going to see a doctor. He tells him all his troubles and, at the end, the doctor says, 'Well, there's only one thing I can recommend: you must go and see the brilliant clown Pagliacci – he'll certainly cheer you up.'

'But, Doctor,' says the sad man, 'that's the trouble: you see, I am Pagliacci . . .'

FUN ADVICE

Always borrow money from a pessimist (they don't expect it back).

Plan to be spontaneous – tomorrow.

Never make eye contact with a tiger.

Live each day as if it were your last – and one day you'll be right.

Never hold a dust buster and a cat at the same time.

Never carry a lightbulb in your back pocket.

Avoid clichés like the plague.

Always remember you're unique, just like everyone else.

Sleep late . . . it's the early worm that gets eaten by the bird.

Never fry food when you're naked.

You are what you eat – so stay away from the jerk chicken.

Wear tight shoes and you'll forget all your other troubles.

FAMILY

Don't judge people by their relatives.
Friends are the family you choose. So do feel free to judge someone by their friends!

Never argue at the dinner table – unless you're not hungry.
Do your bit to make family meals enjoyable.

Don't keep pestering your parents for a new mobile phone.
In fact, don't keep pestering your parents! Though I suspect that children and parents might have different opinions on this one . . .

Whenever a relative sends you a present, make sure you write them a thank-you letter.
It's always appreciated, I promise you.

Ask your parents and grandparents about *their* childhoods, and also about *their* grandparents.
One day you'll want to know all about your family's history, and by then it might be too late.

FRIENDS & ENEMIES

Never say 'Did you get my text/email?'
They did, and they're ignoring you.

Forgive your enemies.
You do this for two reasons – both selfish. Firstly because there is no revenge so complete as forgiveness (they're not going to have the satisfaction of seeing you angry), and secondly because to not forgive them is bad for you and your inner peace. Oh, and by the way, when you forgive your enemies . . . never forget their names.

Let friends help when they offer.
Sometimes you have to learn to take as well as to give.

Never explain – your friends don't need it, and your enemies won't believe you.
Brings to mind that great line: 'Those who matter don't mind and those who mind don't matter.'

Pick your enemies carefully. They're harder to get rid of than friends.

Friends come and go; true enemies remain enemies for life. As proof, consider the fact that no one ever forgets the children who bullied them at school. So think about that if you're ever tempted to bully another child. I've never forgotten the name of the boy who bullied me at school. His name was Ian Stewart and I've never forgiven him. So if you're reading this, Stewart (and, by the way, what are you doing reading a children's book?), I still hate you!

Never interrupt your enemy when they're making a mistake.

Just let them finish and then pounce on them!

Value those friends who make you feel good when you're with them.

They might not be your 'best friends' but they're better for you!

Don't fret about any row or argument you might have with a friend.
Apart from anything, when it comes to rows with friends, you should know the difference between an ordinary friend and a good friend: an ordinary friend thinks the friendship is over when you have a row, whereas the REAL friend knows that it's not a friendship until AFTER you've had a row. By the way, another difference between ordinary and special friends is that an ordinary friend expects you always to be there for them, whereas a REAL friend expects always to be there for you!

Never say 'I told you so' to a friend.
This is the ultimate example of 'do as you would be done by'. Told you!

Never have a friend who treats you like a sidekick.
And don't treat your friends like sidekicks either. And remember, no one needs an entourage.

Don't let good friends drift out of your life.

So easy to do – especially when you move home or change schools. It's worth making the effort to keep in touch with good friends.

JUST DON'T DO IT!

Never kill a ladybird.
It's bad luck – and not just for the ladybird. Besides, just because you can kill something doesn't mean you should.

Never drop litter.
That's what dustbins or, if necessary, pockets are for. Litter is a blight on any community, and just because other idiots have already dropped their litter doesn't give you an excuse to do the same.

Never laugh at anyone's dreams.
Yes, I know it's often tempting – especially if your chubby best friend is boasting about his dream of being the next Usain Bolt, but everyone's entitled to their dreams (and that includes YOU), and it's unkind to rain on their parade. However, there IS a difference between dreams and plans. If your chubby best friend says that he's PLANNING to be the next Usain Bolt and

*tells you he's giving up on his school work
to concentrate on his running, then not only
are you entitled to argue him out of it, you're
OBLIGED to. Real friends believe in your
dreams as much as you do.*

Never run with scissors.
*Yes, I know that this is advice that your
parents and teachers give you, but this
doesn't mean that it doesn't bear repeating!
Similarly, never lick a steak knife.*

Never wear a T-shirt with a 'comedy' phrase on it.

Other people will judge you for it.

Never start a sentence with the words 'Now don't get angry . . .'

Unless you want it to have the opposite effect.

Never buy a book where the cover has the author's name in bigger type than the title of the book.
Most authors' best books are their earlier books. By the time their name gets to be bigger than the title, they're usually trading on their reputations and the books aren't as good.[4]

Don't approach every question with an open mouth.
Unless you want to be a politician when you're older.

Don't type LOL unless you really are laughing out loud.
I prefer 'ha-ha' myself.

Never bother to listen to the loudspeaker messages in the supermarket.
Trust me, they're not for you.

---

4   Note to Editor: Please ensure that my name is smaller than the title on the cover – at least for this book.

Don't eat the silica gel sachets placed in the packaging of electronic equipment.
You'll only do it once . . .

Never use a tool that is more intelligent than you are.

Trouble is, when it comes to DIY – or, indeed, anything practical, EVERY tool is more intelligent than I am.

Never use text message speak unless you're texting.

Your life isn't so busy that you don't have time to write 'you' instead of 'u' or 'are' instead of 'r'.

Never start a statement with the words 'Is it just me, or . . . ?'

It either is just you or it isn't – either way, you're just putting off getting to the point!

Don't even think about Christmas until the beginning of December.

That still gives you more than three weeks of anticipation.

Never say 'No worries' unless you're a native Australian.

The same applies to the Aussie inflection where people raise their tone at the end of sentences.

Don't tell people the ending of movies or books.

<u>I</u> know it's tempting – especially when there's a big twist in the tail – but think how upset you'd be if someone spoiled a book or a film for you. Another example of 'do as you would be done by'.

Don't cycle and listen to music at the same time . . .

Especially if you're going to ask for sympathy when you fall off your bike.

Never go to any party where you'll be the most interesting person there.

By the same token, never THROW a party if you'll be the most interesting person there.

Never channel-surf on Sky during a commercial break.
Every channel has a break at the same time.

Never send on a chain letter.
Bin it.

Never deliberately spread a computer virus.
It might seem like a harmless prank, but it has the potential to cause a lot of distress.

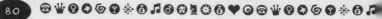

JUST DO IT!

Carry a handkerchief with you.
No one wants to see you sniffing.

Take lots of photos.
One day you'll be really glad you did!

Always give up your seat on the bus or train to a pregnant woman or anyone over seventy.
Do it even if – especially if – no one else on the bus or train is offering, because it is the right thing to do. Having said that, don't automatically assume that any woman with a big belly is pregnant (a recent mistake of mine from which there was no recovering).

Be enthusiastic.
It's appropriate at your age – or indeed at any age!

Go outside every day. Unless you're ill.
Fresh air is invigorating, and sunlight gives you vital Vitamin D.

Keep a daily diary or journal.
You'll be surprised how fascinating you'll find it when you're older.

Never wear a hat or scarf indoors (same goes for sunglasses).
Well, why would you?

Accept a breath mint if someone offers you one.
Well, why do you think they're offering it?

Keep secrets.
Yes, I know it's fun to gossip, but if you've been told something as a secret, then you shouldn't betray that confidence. The key word there is 'betray': repeating a secret is a betrayal of trust, and while it might not matter to you, it almost certainly will to the person who asked you to keep that secret. Incidentally, if a friend tells me a secret and I subsequently cease to be friends with that person, I still consider myself bound to secrecy . . . and so should you!

Save 10 per cent of your pocket money.
You know you should, and you'll be glad that you did!

Lie on your back and look at the stars.
One of the best shows in the world . . . and it's free!

MORE FUN ADVICE

If you really want to know how unimportant you are, try ordering someone else's dog around.

Never eat anything that's bigger than your own head.

When your mum's just had a row with your dad (it happens, it happens), don't let her brush your hair.

If you are willing to admit faults, you have one less fault to admit.

Laugh at your problems; everybody else does.

Never ask your three-year-old brother to hold a tomato.

You can't trust dogs to watch your food.

FOOD & DRINK

Never eat in a restaurant where the toilet is filthy.

If they can't be bothered to clean a part that they know you will see, can you imagine how filthy the other parts (which they know you won't see) are? Like the kitchen . . .

Never buy a hamburger or a hot dog from a stand outside a football ground.
Even if you smother it with ketchup and relish, you're still going to be eating minced-up verrucas and toenails in a bun.

Never pay more than £3 for a portion of chips.
Chippies – i.e. fish and chip shops – will give you a huge portion of chips for half the price you pay at fancy restaurants. Also, chip-shop chips are a lot better for you – lower in fat; higher in vitamins – than the ones you get in burger chains.

MORE FUN ADVICE

Never let any mechanical device know that you are in a hurry.

Never lick a self-adhesive stamp.

Never put both feet in your mouth at the same time, because you won't have a leg to stand on.

Always keep your words soft and sweet – just in case you have to eat them.

Don't sneeze when someone is cutting your hair.

Why buy shampoo when real poo is still free?

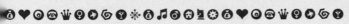

Never wear polka-dot underwear under white shorts.

Don't give your right arm to be ambidextrous.

Never weigh more than your fridge.

Don't worry about the world coming to an end today. It's already tomorrow in Australia.

ADVICE FROM THE DARK SIDE

If you and your friend are being chased by a mad dog, don't worry about out-running

the mad dog, just worry about out-running your friend.

Yes, I know I offered this advice in the introduction, but I repeat it here because it really is the darkest piece of advice I can offer you . . . and yet how true it is! What a pity for me that I would ALWAYS have been out-run by ANY friend . . .

Never believe anything until it has been officially denied.

Believe in mayhem at first sight.

If your sister hits you, don't hit her back. They always catch the second person.

Learn the rules so you know how to break them properly.

Yield to temptation; it may not pass your way again.

Never practise two vices at once.

No matter how hard you try, you can't baptize cats.

Never give up your right to be wrong.

Relax. If it gets too serious, someone else will sort it out.

Never kick a man when he's down; jump on him instead.

Don't take life too seriously (you'll never get out alive anyway).

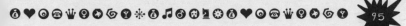

We are responsible for what we do, unless we are celebrities.

Some mistakes are too much fun to only make once.

When trouble arises and things look bad, there is always one individual who perceives a solution and is willing to take command. Very often, that individual is crazy.

Never judge a man until you have walked a mile in his shoes. After that, forget him – you're a mile away and you've got his shoes.

Don't worry about fooling all the people all the time – you need only fool the majority.

Don't take yourself too seriously: no one else does.

If it ain't broke, fix it. If you can't fix it, smash it up.

Always check that everyone else is skinny-dipping before you do.

Never eat anything you can't lift.

Never do tomorrow what you can put off until the day after tomorrow.

If you can't convince them, confuse them.

If you can't learn to do it well, learn to enjoy doing it badly.

Always speak the truth – unless, of course, you are an exceptionally good liar.

Never be too open minded: your brains could fall out.

If getting even doesn't work, then just get odd.

Never squat with your spurs on.

Admit nothing, deny everything and make counter-accusations.

Just do it: it's easier to apologize than it is to get permission.

Never do anything standing that you can do sitting, or anything sitting that you can do lying down.

Do what you *want* to do before you do what you *have* to do.

Take a lesson from the weather: it pays no attention to criticism either.

Never laugh at anyone's dreams unless they're really, *really*, stupid.

Between two evils always pick the one you haven't tried.

If two wrongs don't make a right, try three.

Never get into fights with ugly people: they have nothing to lose.

When you're in over your head, make sure you close your mouth.

If the worst comes to the worst, you can always be a bad example.

GOOD PROVERBIAL ADVICE

Don't let a little dispute injure a great friendship.
Even the best of friends – especially the best of friends! – are going to argue from time to time. The key thing is not to let it get out of hand and ruin the relationship. I've seen great friendships end because of some silly row where neither person was prepared to back down. What a waste!

Time heals almost everything.
Sometimes you just have to give time time.

Never open the door to a lesser evil, for other ones invariably slink in after it.
Once you start, it can be hard to stop. Take racism as an example. One of your friends might think it's harmless to make racist jokes. But once you start judging – and demonizing – people on the basis of their skin-colour or religion, it might not end with a joke but with something far more serious.

Don't buy a whole cow just because you want a pint of milk.

One of my favourite proverbs and one I use an awful lot! Doesn't just apply to cows and milk!

Never trouble trouble till trouble troubles you.

Try saying that when you're tired! Basically, if there's any chance that you might avoid a problem, then do nothing until (and unless) you're actually confronted by that problem.

Never try to walk across a river just because it has an average depth of one metre.

The key word here is 'average': it might be two metres in some places. However, I think this proverb is also encouraging us in a more general way to pay attention to the sort of detail that could be vital.

Don't spur a willing horse.

Doesn't just apply to horses! If someone is doing their very best, there's no point in screaming at them to do better. In fact, it might even be counter-productive.

Never wear your best trousers when you go out to fight for freedom.

Lovely proverb that probably requires some explanation. When you're going out to do

something really important, you don't want to have to worry about your clothes getting ruined – or, indeed, about anything else. In other words, you want to be able to give it your best shot. Obviously doesn't apply to occasions – e.g. weddings, official ceremonies, etc. – where you DO have to wear your best trousers . . .

Live out of your imagination, not your history.

Even if you've failed at something before, you shouldn't be put off trying again.

Always drink upstream from the herd.

Obviously it's better to drink uncontaminated water – and sit in a better section of the aeroplane. Sadly, for any number of reasons, it might not always be possible, and we might indeed have to be part of the herd. Still, it doesn't hurt to have ambition . . .

Never test the depth of the water with both feet.

Don't fully commit yourself until you have at least tested the water. And, yes, once again, this doesn't just apply to water!

When you lose, don't lose the lesson.
Which is a slightly strained way of saying that with defeats and setbacks comes experience and, from there, wisdom. If you don't learn from that experience, then

you're not going to acquire wisdom.

If three people say you are an ass, put on a bridle.

It's a proverb – not an instruction. Basically, what it means is that we're not always the best judge of ourselves – especially in the heat of the moment. So if you're playing with friends and three of them tell you that you're being unreasonable, then you're being unreasonable.

Dig your well before you're thirsty.

There are lots of proverbs to this effect – another one I like is 'Fix your roof while the sun shines.' In other words, make sure you do the things that have to be done in good time and not at the very last minute when you've no choice as to the timing.

Better to light a candle than to curse the darkness.

The fact is that the solution to a problem is often so easy that you wonder whether some people would simply rather complain than do anything about it.

Choose an author as you choose a friend.
In other words, look out for the same qualities as you do when you're making friends with someone. Are they (or, more importantly, their books) someone who won't let you down? Do you share a sense of humour or a set of values? Will you want to spend time with them? Will the books be of a consistently high standard (i.e. not let you down)? You can see the point of the proverb!

Wait until it is night before saying that it has been a fine day.
Don't tempt fate! My version of this would be: 'Wait until the end of a car journey before remarking on how light the traffic was' – because if you don't, then sure as eggs is eggs, you'll end up in a traffic jam!

Judge your success by what you had to give up in order to get it.
Particularly applies to sportspeople and musicians.

Tell your friend a lie. If he keeps it secret, then tell him the truth.
Well, it's a risk-free way of discovering whether your friend can be trusted!

Better to be alone than in bad company.
Don't be afraid of being on your own: you can often have a very enjoyable time – certainly more so than if you're with people you don't like. How often do we yearn for a good book when we're with boring people!

The cheapest is the dearest.
Clearly this isn't always true: in fact, very often the cheapest is just that – the cheapest! However, sometimes, taking the cheap option might involve you in long-term costs so, in that way, it can be the more/most expensive option.

Cross the stream where it is shallowest.
Er, obviously! Though this might be a metaphor for working – identifying the easiest option and taking it.

Think before speaking.

Fine advice . . . and one day I'll try to adopt it myself.

If you want a thing well done, do it yourself.
*Not always possible (or even desirable),
but if you can do something yourself, then
you should – not because you'll necessarily
do it better but because you will at least do
it to your own satisfaction.*

Keep your mouth shut and your ears open.
*Be a good listener. Your ears will never get
you in trouble.*

Live and let live.
*NOT to be confused with the James Bond
book/film Live and Let Die! Enjoy your
life and let other people – and creatures –
enjoy theirs . . . even if you don't
necessarily agree with their lifestyles.*

Never take what you cannot use.
*I'm told by my wife that I should remember
this the next time we find ourselves at an
all-you-can-eat buffet . . .*

Look before you leap, but, having leaped, never look back.

The first part of this proverb – look before you leap – is obvious and was, I thought, the whole proverb, but it turns out that there's an extra bit about not looking back. I suppose it's fair enough: once we've made our checks and done whatever we

have to do, then there's probably no point in looking back – we certainly can't change anything – and it's true that it's important to keep focused on the task ahead. I know it's a good thing to be that single-minded, but you can't blame someone for looking back and reassuring themselves: it's only human!

...eryday decisions from the head but ...cisions from the heart.

...t you feel matters more than what you think when it comes to the important stuff. Learn to trust your instincts.

Never write what you dare not sign.

If you're going to write or say something, don't do it anonymously. Especially applies to graffiti – so DON'T DO IT.

Don't regret what you do, regret what you didn't do.

Doesn't apply to eating and drinking, where the opposite is almost always the case.

Never worry about the future. It comes soon enough.

Please note that there's an important difference between 'worrying' about the future and planning for it.

Of two evils choose the lesser.

Sometimes you're in a situation where you have to choose between two courses of action – neither desirable. Perhaps you're torn between watching a friend doing something bad (on the one hand) and telling on them (on the other). Neither course of action feels good, so you just have to take the 'less-bad' one: telling on them for their own good.

Ask the experienced rather than the learned.

A person who has actually been through something – like fighting in a war, for example – knows more about it than someone who has merely studied it.

He who does not ask will never get a bargain.

Well, it doesn't hurt, does it? And you never know till you ask if you can get a reduction. The key thing is to do it courteously and with charm: if you demand a lower price, you'll only put the salesperson's back up and they won't budge.

Give respect where respect is due.

Another one of those proverbs that boils down to 'Do as you would be done by.'

Share your knowledge. It's a way to achieve immortality.

Alas (from my point of view), this probably doesn't apply to trivia . . .

Don't burn your bridges.

You'd be surprised how many times you have to cross the same river.

Neither a lender nor a borrower be.
And before you borrow money from a friend, decide which you need more.

Never cut what can be untied.
It's worth taking a little extra time to untie something so that it can be reused – even if tearing it open or cutting it is easier. Applies to cereal packets, which can be refastened if you can be bothered to open them properly.

Take people as you find them.
Don't automatically expect everyone to be just like you – and don't try to change them.

Judge a man by his questions rather than his answers.
Applies to women too (proverbs are old-fashioned like that!).

Don't wash your dirty linen in public.
There's no need to tell everybody about your most intimate secrets. Similarly, consider the proverb 'Don't wear your

heart on your sleeve': by all means be in touch with your feelings but don't go over the top. Just be appropriate.

If you're riding ahead of the herd, take a look back every now and then to make sure it's still there.
Often there's a narrow line between (on the one hand) leading a group and (on the other) going off on your own. It's not that one is worse than the other, but they are different, and you should know which of the two you are doing.

A fair face may hide a foul heart.
In other words, don't be misled by a person's looks – good or bad. Remember too that beauty is skin-deep but ugliness goes right down to the bone.

Burn not your house to rid it of the mouse.
Don't overreact! If there's a problem, do what you have to do to get rid of it . . . but no more than you have to do. After all, you wouldn't take a sledgehammer to crack a nut, would you?

When you want to be noticed, do more than is expected.

Only applies to getting noticed in a good way! Go the extra mile. If your mum asks you to put the dirty dishes in the sink, don't just do that – wash them up too. And then dry them and put them away. That'll get you noticed (in a good way!). It'll also mean that the next time you do something a little naughty, your mum will be more likely to overlook it.

Don't believe all you hear, spend all you have or sleep all you want.

Some, some and some. Not everything you hear will be true (so don't believe it all); if you spend ALL your money, you won't have any left (er, obviously); sleep as much as you like – but only SOMETIMES: if you always sleep as much as you want, you won't have much time left to do everything else.

Be open-minded, but not empty-headed.

Most people pride themselves on being

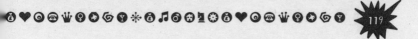

open-minded but many of them don't guard against empty-headedness. We should all try to be open-minded about any thing or subject for as long as it takes us to evaluate the worth/honesty/truth of that thing or subject. Some subjects – like racism – don't require us to be open-minded at all: we can all agree, right from the off, that racism (discriminating against people on the basis of their skin colour or nationality) is a bad thing. Other things require longer consideration, but when you've reached a conclusion, then to carry on being open-minded is not an option.

Never interrupt when you are being flattered.

If someone's telling you how wonderful you are – we should all be so lucky! – let them finish. Don't interrupt to tell them that they've got it wrong or that you're not worthy of such kind words. The truth is, we get flattered so rarely that we just have to make the most of it. So savour each second and keep your mouth shut until the very end. Then you can go into your 'Oh, don't be silly!' routine or, much better, just say 'Thanks'! Bear in mind, however, that it's better to be praised than it is to be flattered.

Mind your own business, but watch out for others'.

'Mind your own business' works on two levels (usually): keep your nose out of things that don't concern you; and (less common) look after the things that matter to you. The second part of this proverb – which, I confess, I'd never heard of – doesn't contradict the first part. All it means is that while you shouldn't be nosy or pry, you also have a responsibility to keep an eye out for other people in case they need help. It's all about YOUR intentions: are you looking at other people's business for YOUR sake (and curiosity) or for THEIR sake (and wellbeing).

In matters of style, swim with the current; in matters of principle, stand like a rock.

When it comes to fashion – which doesn't

matter – it doesn't hurt to go along with everyone else (i.e. go with the flow); however, when it comes to important things like principles – which DO matter – you must stick to your guns. Some might argue that you don't need to swim with the current over stylish matters – and they'd be right – but I think the point of the proverb is that if you 'stand like a rock' over smaller matters (like style), then it won't mean as much when you do so over bigger matters (like principles).

DON'T CONFUSE . . .

. . . **comfort with happiness.**

. . . wealth with success.

. . . **age with maturity.**

. . . an apology with an excuse.

NEVER UNDERESTIMATE . . .

. . . the power of stupid people in large groups.

. . . your friend's ability to get you into more trouble.

. . . your power to change yourself (but never *over*estimate your power to change others).

. . . the power of jealousy.

. . . the capacity of another person to have exactly the same shortcomings as you have.

. . . your ability to deal with any problem.

NEVER BE AFRAID TO . . .

. . . try something new.

. . . say what you think.

. . . raise your hand in class.

. . . do what's right.

. . . look stupid.

. . . go to the dentist.

. . . laugh at yourself.

. . . make friends with the new child in the class.

. . . stick up for what you believe in.

. . . ask questions.

NEVER PICK YOUR NOSE AFTER...

. . . chopping chillies.

. . . eating a kebab.

. . . touching jalapeño peppers.

. . . you've just wiped your bottom.

NEVER TRUST . . .

. . . **people who don't move their arms when they walk.**

. . . a man who can't stop whistling.

. . . **a man with a comb-over – if he can lie to himself that he has a full head of hair, then he can lie to you too.**

. . . people who call themselves 'happy bunnies'.

. . . **a grown man who calls himself Timmy instead of Timothy or Jimbo instead of James.**

. . . a man with a goatee beard.

. . . **a skinny chef.**

. . . experts.

. . . **a balding man with a ponytail.**

. . . a film trailer.

. . . anyone who doesn't like dogs.

. . . anyone with more than three cats.

. . . people who tell you all their troubles but never share any of their happiness with you.

. . . a Rottweiler owner who tells you that their dog never bites.

. . . a politician with two eyes, two ears, a nose and a mouth.

. . . a man who tucks his shirt into his underpants.

THE DARWIN AWARDS

are an extremely funny invention to 'honour those who do a service to humanity by permanently removing themselves from the gene pool'. In other words, here are – or were – some of the biggest idiots on the planet.

Here are some past deeds which have been 'recognized' by the judges.

Do I need to add anything else – except for the well-worn words: 'Don't try this at home'?

An American woman was driving a convertible car with the roof off down the highway when she decided to swap seats with her passenger. But where anyone else would have stopped the car first, this woman decided to do it while the car was going at top speed. Alas, she slipped and fell out onto the road, where she promptly died.

A Brazilian man installed a tiny electric fence around his car to protect it against the frequent robberies that occurred in his neighbourhood. Unfortunately for him, he forgot that he had left the fence on and suffered an electric shock that killed him.

An American motorist stopped for a beer and then got back into his car – only to find himself in a traffic jam.

It would have been OK, but he was soon in need of a pee. So he got out of his car and jumped over the low concrete wall by the side of the road . . . only to fall 20 metres to his death. The poor fellow thought there was another road on the other side of the wall – but there wasn't.

A German man was alone in an underground carriage in Berlin when he decided it would be a brilliant idea to smash one of the windows. By swinging feet forward from a handrail into the window, he not only managed to break the glass but also succeeded in being sucked

out of the moving train, and was left dead on the tracks.

Greensboro, North Carolina, was deluged with rain, and several cars were stranded on flooded roads, but one woman wasn't deterred. She hopped on her moped and drove to a convenience store, where she 'possibly had a beer' (according to her mother) before deciding to blunder home through the storm. She phoned home to say, 'My moped has two rubber wheels, Mom – I'll be fine.'

The Highway Patrol had blocked off several roads that were inundated with water, including the woman's route home. But she rode right past the officer and the barriers, lost control of her vehicle, and fell into the swollen creek below. The officer retrieved a rope from his vehicle and proceeded to haul her out of the water.

He then interviewed the woman, probably asking her why she was speeding through a roadblock during a flash flood. When the

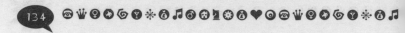

officer returned to his patrol car to call for assistance, the woman took the opportunity to escape – by jumping back into the creek to rescue her beloved moped.

The officer attempted to rescue her again, but alas, it was too late.

Annoyed at how slowly her boyfriend was driving, an American woman nagged him to go faster so she could get to work on time. Joking that it would be faster for her to walk to work, she opened the door of the pickup truck and stuck her foot out before falling to her death.

An American woman was visiting a lake with a friend. Recent bouts of heavy rain had resulted in a flood of runoff water, and so they decided it would be fun to take a ride on a mattress that happened to be careening down the surging water.

Unfortunately, it was a foam, egg-crate style mattress pad. Imagine a wet foam pad. Are you sinking yet? The poor woman

simply vanished from sight. The next morning her body was found in a tangle of trees several miles away.

WORDS AND PHRASES TO AVOID

''Ave it!'

'It's not rocket science.'

'For sure' (instead of yes).

'Less' when you mean 'fewer'.

'Fewer' when you mean 'less'.

'Don't give up the day job.'

'Get a life.'

'Tell me about it . . .'

'I'm loving it.'

'Been there, done that.'

'Doin' me 'ead in.'

'Listen up.'

'At this point in time . . .'

'Who rattled your cage, then?'

'You know . . .'

'What are you like!'

'Whatever . . .'

'Simples!'

'Like . . .'

PRONUNCIATIONS TO AVOID

'Burgalry' for burglary.

'Ex cetera' for et cetera.

'Haitch' for h.

'Noo' for new.

'Sickth' for sixth.

'Ter' for to.

'But-er' for butter.

'Fink' for think.

'Uzz' for us.

'Eng-er-land' for England.

IF AT FIRST YOU DON'T SUCCEED . . .

If at first you don't succeed, try again and then give up.

If at first you don't succeed, try again and then give up and pay someone else to do it.

If at first you don't succeed, try, try again. Then quit. There's no use being a fool about it.

If you try and don't succeed, cheat. Repeat until caught. Then lie.

If at first you don't succeed, destroy all evidence that you tried.

If at first you don't succeed, skydiving is not for you.

GREAT TRUTHS

You will make many mistakes in your life, but you won't be a failure until and unless you start blaming other people for them.
There's nothing wrong with making mistakes – they're the price we pay for living – but you must take responsibility for them.

No one can make you feel inferior without your consent.
It takes two people to make you feel inferior or small: the person doing it, and you for not stopping them before, during or after.

The time will never be *just* right.
Sometimes you just have to go for it.

Some people would rather be certain they're miserable than risk being happy.
You just have to take a chance.

The only really decent thing to do behind a person's back is pat it.

I take the view that you should always be nicer about a person when they're not there to defend themselves. At least if you say something challenging to a person's face, they have the chance to explain or apologize.

You can't skip and be unhappy at the same time.

Same applies to playing the ukulele.

Winners do what losers don't want to do.

Or simply aren't prepared to do – like dedicate themselves to what it takes to win (training hard, denying themselves treats like sweets, missing out on a social life, etc.).

No one has a finer command of language than the person who keeps their mouth shut.

There's the added benefit that, if you keep your mouth shut, you'll never put your foot in it.

The person who knows how to laugh at himself will never cease to be amused.
I never cease to laugh at myself – but that's probably because my whole life is like a situation comedy!

No amount of belief makes something a fact.
The more you're obliged to believe in something to make it real, the less likely it is to be a genuine fact.

A much cleverer reply will always occur to you immediately after you click the 'Send' button.

Same goes with the end of a telephone conversation. You always think of what you should have said/written/texted afterwards. In fact, there's even an expression for it: 'l'esprit de l'escalier' – which translates from French as 'the spirit (or wit) of the staircase'. Why? Well, because in the old days, rich people had their lounges – or 'drawing rooms' – on the first floor, so you'd think of that brilliant line or witty riposte on your way out . . . down the staircase. So the next time someone says, 'Oh, if only I'd thought of it at the time!' you can say, 'Ah, l'esprit de l'escalier.'

It is almost impossible to smile on the outside without feeling better on the inside.

Well, it's worth a try, isn't it?

Tact is the ability to describe others as they see themselves.
It's also the art of making a point without making an enemy.

Having too much can be as bad as having too little.
Applies to everything from money to (especially) sweets and chocolates.

Life is 10 per cent what happens to you and 90 per cent how you react to it.
OK, the proportions might shift, but you get the general drift that it's your response to events that really counts.

What you do now will create memories for when you're older.
Good or bad memories, but you WILL remember the things you do in childhood – especially the really embarrassing things. Sorry to tell you this, but it happens to be true!

Not getting precisely what you want is sometimes the best thing that can happen to you.

The reverse is also true: getting precisely what you want is often the worst thing that can happen to you. Applies especially to extremely spoiled children at Christmas time.

If you can solve your problem, then what's the use in worrying? If you can't solve it, then what's the use in worrying?

I guess it's only worth worrying if the worrying itself helps you to solve the problem.

Better to be occasionally cheated than to be constantly suspicious.

This is SO true. There are people – not all of them old ladies – who really do think that the world is always trying to cheat them, and so they'll always check their change and query every bill. And you know what? Yes, occasionally they will find there's been a mistake and, yes, it wasn't in their favour – but does that justify a lifetime of suspicion?

I don't think so. I tend to trust people – unless they give me good reason not to – and I don't think I'm any poorer as a result. What's for certain is that I'm a lot happier than I would be if I suspected everyone of being a potential thief or cheat. And I wonder about people who are constantly mistrustful: are they as honest and decent as they are suspicious? If they find that a mistake has been made in their favour, do they point it out? If they're being consistent, they should. For myself, although I'm not a great checker, if I do discover that I've been given too much change, I always point it out. After all, I'd say something if I happened to notice that I'd been underpaid, so I have a responsibility to act when the opposite happens.

Absolute certainty is the greatest illusion of all.

Beware of people who are absolutely certain of everything. I have a good pal who's like that and I sometimes say to him, 'I wish I were as certain about anything as you are about everything!'

You can't achieve the impossible unless you attempt the absurd.

This is another way of saying you've got to 'think outside the box' if you're trying to solve a particularly difficult – not to say impossible – problem. I like the idea that great advances in science don't happen when scientists shout 'Eureka!' but, rather, when they say, 'Now, that's funny . . .'

A clear conscience never fixed anything.

Sounds like advice from the dark side, but there is a truth here: sometimes, in order to do something that really has to be done, you're obliged to do something unpalatable along the way. Winning the Second World War occasionally required men to do things – like bombing civilians – that would weigh on their consciences later in life, but it was vital at the time in order to defeat a greater evil.

Just because you say so doesn't mean it's true.

Sometimes you have to be able to provide proof.

Behold the turtle who makes progress only when he sticks his neck out.

I love this saying because it conjures up such a wonderful image. Sometimes we have to take risks in order to achieve things and, yes, like the turtle, we have to stick our necks out.

If you're not the lead dog, the scenery never changes.

Leadership carries many responsibilities but it has its rewards!

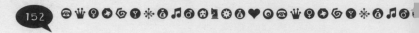

In order to get a bank loan, you must first prove that you don't need one.

Or to put it another way, banks will lend you an umbrella on any day except when it's raining.

Justice is when the decision is in your favour.

I have a theory about this. Some people (adults and children) have a strong sense of injustice: they howl if a decision goes against them or if they're blamed for something they didn't do. However, they don't have an equally strong sense of injustice when the decision goes for them when it shouldn't have done. You see this sometimes in sport: competitors may complain bitterly when they feel they're right but are curiously silent when they're in the wrong and someone else is getting the blame.

You may have to fight a battle more than once to win it.

Applies to exams (i.e. retakes) and addictions as much as it does to warfare: the point is, sometimes you don't win first time around – you just have to persevere.

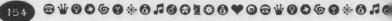

If you want the rainbow, you've got to put up with the rain.

Everything has its price, but if you want something enough, then you'll put up with it.

You learn when you're young; you understand when you're old.

There's an old French saying that translates as: 'If the young only knew; if the old only could.' I knew lots of stuff when I was younger, but I really wish I'd been capable of understanding it as well as I do now! Consider also the proverb, 'The young men know the rules but the old men know the exceptions.'

Art is never finished, only abandoned.

At some point, the writer, artist, sculptor or film-maker has to say, 'OK, it's done.'

Right is right, even if everyone is against it; and wrong is wrong, even if everyone is for it.

You have to stick up for what's right – whatever anyone else says – but before you insist that you're right and they're wrong, have another think: it could be that they're right after all.

Kindness is more important than wisdom.

As I've said elsewhere, I really do believe

that kindness is the most important quality
(and the most underrated virtue) that
a human being can possess. So it's no
wonder that I rate it even more highly than
wisdom. In fact, you could even say that
the understanding of the fact that kindness
is more important than wisdom is itself the
beginning of wisdom. By that token, you
can't do a kindness too soon, for you never
know how soon it will be too late.

If you can dream it, you can do it.
This DOESN'T apply to dreams you have
when asleep but to dreams – or aspirations
– you have when awake. I don't want
anyone jumping off a cliff top because they
had a dream they could fly . . .

You may not realize it when it happens, but a kick in the teeth may be the best thing in the world for you.

I think we're talking metaphorically . . . as in a setback, not a real tooth-loosening, gum-shattering, literal kick in the teeth.

Time is the most valuable thing you can spend.
It's also the most valuable gift you can give to someone – so long as you let them spend your time the way they want to.

Whenever you find yourself on the side of the majority, it's worth taking time to reconsider.
Well, it can't hurt to rethink the issue and your position on it.

The person who can read books but doesn't has no advantage over the person who can't read at all.
It's not what you CAN do but what you DO do.

There are only two ways of telling the complete truth – anonymously and posthumously.
This applies to the complete truth on extremely contentious issues: obviously it doesn't mean that you should ONLY tell the truth anonymously and posthumously!

There are no short cuts to any place worth going.

In fact, the very existence of a short cut might mean that the place is not really worth going to.

161

It's much more impressive when others discover your good qualities without your help.
Even though it can be achingly tempting to prompt them!

There is nothing worse than aggressive stupidity.
Especially when exercised by loud, aggressively stupid people in large groups.

The first step to getting the things you want out of life is to decide what you want.
I mean really want . . . This doesn't apply to new mobile phones or other gadgets, but to important things like career choices and serious challenges.

Nothing is ever as simple as we hope it will be.
But nor is it usually as terrible as we fear it might be.

There is nothing more frightening than ignorance in action.

Especially when perpetrated by someone in a position of authority – like a parent.

It is harder to conceal ignorance than to acquire knowledge.
So you might as well learn.

A free society is one where it is safe to be unpopular.
That's what makes Britain such a great country: the tolerance extended to people who are stupid, wrong or simply disagree with the majority.

A weekend wasted isn't a wasted weekend.
Some of my favourite weekends have been spent doing absolutely nothing but reading, walking, eating and chatting.

Life isn't fair.
Get used to it.

Everybody is somebody else's weirdo.
This obviously doesn't apply to the author.[5]

---

5   Editor's note: this ESPECIALLY applies to the author.

Anybody who thinks money will make you happy hasn't got money.
When you've got money, you soon find that happiness depends on other things like health, friendship and peace of mind. However, there is something in the thought that although money won't make you happy, it'll pay for the search.

If you want to make peace, you don't talk to your friends; you talk to your enemies.
A lesson for individuals as well as governments.

No act of kindness, no matter how small, is ever wasted.
Even if you don't profit by it (in material terms), you still gain from it spiritually.

Eighty per cent of success is showing up.
Very true. When you're starting out, you want to believe that it's all down to talent, but in fact consistency and reliability are far more prized by employers.

If you're going to walk on thin ice you might as well dance.

Please, please, PLEASE don't take this literally – though it is the most wonderful metaphor.

Life can only be understood backwards, but it must be lived forwards.
In other words, look at life through the windscreen, not the rear-view mirror.

Extremes meet.
That's why fascists and communists have so much in common.

What may be done at any time will be done at no time.
You really do have to timetable your chores or duties or they simply won't get done at all.

Nothing is really work unless you would rather be doing something else.
That's why they call it work and not play.

Bad is never good until worse happens.
So true. There you are, bemoaning your life, when something REALLY bad happens that makes you think, 'Oh, how wonderful life would be if only that hadn't happened.'

Luck is where opportunity meets preparation.
So if you've prepared and you're given the opportunity, make sure you act upon it.

The best armour is to keep out of range.
Doesn't just apply to warfare.

A closed mind is like a closed book.
Don't be TOO certain about everything.

An army of sheep led by a lion would defeat an army of lions led by a sheep.
Leadership is everything!

Gossip is the most destructive force in the universe.
So why does it make the world go round?

Envy is the ulcer of the soul.
Don't succumb to it yourself – and avoid anyone who suffers from it.

If you lend someone £10 and never see that person again, it was probably worth it.
Hence the expression 'It's better to give than it is to lend, and it costs about the same'.

This applies double to friends and relatives. A gift makes both of you feel good – and there's just as much chance of the recipient repaying it as they would if it were a loan. The difference is that you don't lie awake seething about it.

What other people think of you is none of your business.
All you can do is be your best; from there, you have no control of what people make of that.

Compromise is the art of dividing a cake so that everybody believes that he or she got the biggest piece.
When cutting up cakes or dividing something in half, the cutter or divider should always allow the other person first pick.

Cats only like you when they want something.
Which is probably why I don't like 'em!

You always enjoy a song more when you're singing along.
Standing on the sidelines is never as much fun as playing. Get involved whenever possible!

Returning violence for violence multiplies violence.
Sometimes you have no choice, but where you do have a choice, you should exercise it with caution.

Home is the place where, when you have to go there, they have to take you in.
Home is also where you can say anything you like because nobody listens to you anyway.

There should always be time for courtesy.
It's a small thing but it's important.

The only thing necessary for the triumph of evil is for good people to do nothing.
When bad things are happening, it's not enough to simply not participate: you have an obligation to stand up and do something (the only exception to that rule is if interfering would lead to you getting physically hurt).

The person who knows how to laugh at himself will never cease to be amused.
You're funnier than you think, you know (especially when you can't see the joke).

Generosity is giving more than you can; pride is taking less than you need.
I recommend both . . . in moderation.

A wise person can see more from the bottom of a well than a fool can from a mountain top.

Though there's no reason why the wise person shouldn't visit a mountain top.

The brain that doesn't feed itself eats itself.
We all have to keep on learning.

He who hesitates is probably right.
Contradicts the proverb 'He who hesitates is lost,' and is probably a lot truer.

You never want the one you can afford.
Or afford the one you want.

Timing has an awful lot to do with the outcome of a rain dance.
Keep on dancing, and eventually it will rain.

You can't go back and start a new beginning, but you can start creating a new ending right now.
You can control your future a lot better than your past . . . and there IS such a thing as redemption.

The person who says they're willing to meet you halfway is usually a poor judge of distance.
That's me, by the way. My friends know that my idea of halfway means a few miles

from my home – no matter how far they have to travel.

If you think your teacher's tough, wait till you get a boss.
A lot of people offered me this advice when I was at school, but in truth, I've never encountered anyone quite as fearsome as Mr Bromhead, my school history teacher.

No good music ever came blaring out of a car.
Oi, you – TURN IT DOWN!

Most of the time what you are looking for is right in front of you.
Doesn't necessarily apply to keys or television remote controls.

There is NO such thing as a genuine medium or psychic. They're either crooks or deluded.

Don't just take my word for it – check out Derren Brown, who can replicate ANYTHING any medium or psychic claims to be able to do.

Sandwiches bought in petrol stations will always disappoint.
And the more 'exotic' the filling, the more they'll disappoint.

Freedom is not worth having if it doesn't include the freedom to make mistakes.
This advice really applies more to parents than it does to their children. As a father, I had to learn that giving my children the freedom to go off and do things on their own also meant giving them the freedom to do things that I would rather they didn't do. But unless I trusted them – and they saw that I trusted them – then they would never learn to do the right things. Or, in the words of another great truth: If you don't learn from your mistakes, then you will repeat them.

In a supermarket, the other queues always move faster than yours.
Or does it just seem that way?

Everything takes longer than you think.
Well, not EVERYTHING, but things that

matter to you do. You should always allow more time than you think you'll need.

No one is great if they think they are.
Part of what makes great people great is the fact that they themselves don't see it.

It's better to make too much pasta than too little.
Same goes for rice.

The clothes you like best in the sale are never in your size.
Well, they're never in MY size!

'Bad' foods are more enjoyable than 'good' ones.
But not half an hour later . . .

Cats always jump onto the lap of someone who hates cats – no matter how many cat lovers there are in the room.
They know, you know!

Whenever you make a journey by bicycle, it's always more uphill than downhill.
Especially when you're nearing the end.

No child ever throws up in the toilet.

I write with the experience of someone who was a child and is also the father of children . . .

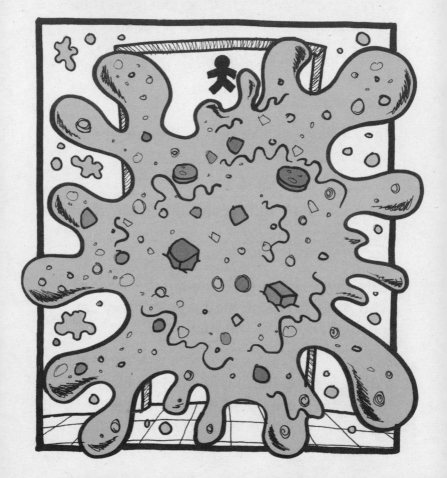

Anything that happens enough times to irritate you will happen at least once more.
Especially applies to irritating things done by friends.

Gluttony isn't a secret vice.
If you eat too much – especially too much of the wrong foods – it WILL eventually show!

Nothing is as easy as it looks.
Especially applies when lots of people are watching you mess up.

Swallowing angry words is easier than having to eat them.
A nice way of saying that you should think twice – and then think again – before saying something horrible just because you're in a bad mood.

No one is in charge of your happiness but you.
Don't rely on other people to make you happy – ultimately it's up to/down to YOU.

Beauty is only skin-deep but ugliness goes right to the bone.

One of my favourite sayings – and how often a beautiful-looking person turns out to be truly ugly when you get to know them . . . On the other hand, you might think it doesn't matter if beauty is just skin-deep. What do you want – beautiful intestines?

If you shoot for the moon and miss, you're still among the stars.

Aim high, and who knows what you might achieve.

It takes longer to lose weight than it did to put it on.

I write from bitter experience . . .

Sometimes the best helping hand you can give is a good firm push.

It depends on the person, but there are times when a friend needs a little tough love.

The key to failure is trying to please everybody.

Do what's right – or what you really have to do – and you'll please enough people . . . or, at least, the RIGHT people.

Genius does what it must, talent does what it can, and the rest of us had best do what we're told.

And neither you nor I are geniuses . . .

It's better to be envied than it is to be pitied.

Almost NOTHING is worse than being pitied, but even so, you still don't want to be envied.

It's better to understand a little than to misunderstand a lot.

It's not how much you know but how well you understand it.

A compliment is sometimes better than the truth.

So when your spotty elder sister or brother

asks you about their complexion, tell them how much you like their haircut instead.

The hardness of butter is directly proportional to the softness of the bread.
Or does it just seem that way?

Tilting at windmills hurts you more than the windmills.
Which is true, but sometimes you should still tilt at them anyway.

Climate is what you expect; weather is what you get.
Especially in Britain, where you can never rely on the weather to be anything but unpredictable.

If you do what you've always done, you'll get what you've always got.
Sometimes you have to break out of your comfort zone and really stretch yourself.

FUN TRUTHS

You can tune a piano, but you can't tuna fish.

If it wasn't for the last minute, nothing would ever get done.

A clean desk is a sign of a cluttered desk drawer.

A torch is a case for holding dead batteries.

Give me ambiguity or give me something else.

All generalizations are false, including this one.

If you read a lot of books, you're considered well-read. But if you watch a lot of TV, you're not considered well-viewed.

Stamps which don't stick when you want them to will stick to other things when you don't want them to.

Of all the noises known to man, opera is the most expensive.

It's bad luck to be superstitious (think about it).

41.7 per cent of all statistics are made up on the spot.

Poetry is living proof that rhyme doesn't pay.

When you dial a wrong number, it's never engaged.

Whoever said that nothing is impossible never tried slamming a revolving door.

One way to stop a runaway horse is to bet on it.

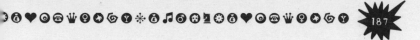

If God had really intended men to fly, he'd have made it easier to get to – and through – the airport.

The worst book in a trilogy is the fourth.

Anyone who claims to be in control of every aspect of their lives has obviously never needed to sneeze halfway through a poo.

Only two groups of people fall for flattery – men and women.

Friendly fire isn't – and nor are foolproof plans.

If you look like your passport photo, you're too ill to travel.

Laughing at our mistakes can lengthen our own life. Laughing at someone else's can shorten it.

Everyone is in awe of the lion tamer in a cage with half a dozen lions. Everyone, that is, except the school bus driver.

There is no time like the pleasant.

The early bird may get the worm, but the second mouse gets the cheese.

Neither teenagers nor cats turn their heads when you call them by name.

189

TRUTHS FROM THE DARK SIDE

No problem is so large or so difficult that it can't be blamed on somebody else.

Anybody who hates cats can't be all bad.

Friends come and go but enemies accumulate.

Expect the worst, and you'll never be disappointed.

If everything seems to be going well, you have obviously overlooked something.

Those who live by the sword get shot by those who don't.

If the enemy is in range, so are you.

The hidden flaw never remains hidden for ever.

There is always one more imbecile than you counted on.

Conscience is the inner voice that warns us somebody may be looking.

That which does not kill me had better be able to run away very fast.

There are three types of men: the ones who learn by reading; the few who learn by observation; and then there are the ones who have to pee on the electric fence for themselves.

Laughter's the best medicine – unless you're diabetic, and then it's insulin.

Junk is something you've kept for years and throw away two weeks before you need it.

A clear conscience is usually the sign of a bad memory.

Anything worth taking seriously is worth making fun of.

The better the Sunday, the worse the Monday.

Some people are like Slinkies – not really good for anything, but you still can't help but smile when you see one tumble down the stairs.

If you can keep your head when all around you are losing theirs, you obviously don't understand the severity of the situation.

Anything worth taking seriously is worth making fun of.

The odds of the bread falling butter-side

down are directly proportional to the value of the carpet.

Artificial intelligence is no match for natural stupidity.

Anything you lose automatically doubles in value.

It's not the bullet with your name on it that you need to worry about; it's the thousand others addressed: 'To whom it may concern.'

It may be that the race is not always to the swift, nor the battle to the strong – but that's the way to bet.

Exceptions always outnumber rules.

If you don't remember it, it didn't happen.

If it's not going to plan, maybe there never _was_ a plan.

When the pin is pulled, Mr Grenade is not our friend.

The difference between genius and

stupidity is that genius has its limits.

Any fool can tell the truth, but it requires a clever person to know how to lie well.

The best way to get a small fortune is to start with a large one . . .

If at first you don't succeed . . . you're running about average.

The only substitute for good manners is fast reflexes.

A lone amateur built the Ark; a large group of professionals built the *Titanic*.

If you are going to go to all the trouble of lying, there's no point in being half-hearted about it.

Opportunity may knock only once, but temptation leans on the doorbell.

A conscience is what hurts when the rest of you feels so good.

You'll never really learn to swear until you learn to drive.

Honesty is the best policy, but insanity is the better defence.

It's lonely at the top, but you eat better.

Make it idiot proof, and someone will make a better idiot.

Hard work never killed anyone, but why risk it?

Any acquaintance who calls you 'mate' has forgotten your name.

There's no point in being grown up if you can't be childish sometimes.

Tattoos are easier to get than they are to get rid of.

You don't stop playing because you grow old; you grow old because you stop playing.

You need only two tools – WD-40 and duct tape. If it doesn't move and it should, use WD-40. If it moves and it shouldn't, use the tape.

The difference between school and life is that in school, you're taught a lesson and then given a test, whereas in life, you're given a test that teaches you a lesson.

By the time you realize that maybe your parents were right after all, you'll probably have a child who thinks – *or knows* – that *you're* wrong.

You're a success as an adult if you get up in the morning and go to bed at night, and in between you've done what you want to do.

It doesn't matter how many times you get knocked down, but how many times you get up.

You can't win the lottery if you don't buy a ticket – as the following joke illustrates:

Mike really wanted to win the lottery. So he goes to church and says to God, 'Oh Lord, help me win the lottery. If only I won the lottery, how happy I would be. And just think of all the good I could do if only I had the money!'

Of course, nothing happens, and so, the following week, Mike's back in church once again asking God to help him win the lottery.

Again, he doesn't win, so the next week

he's really bending God's ear, when suddenly he hears a voice from the heavens:

'Mike, do me a favour!'

'What is it, God?'

'Meet me halfway.'

'How?'

'Buy a ticket!'

However, never buy more than ONE ticket. One ticket buys the dream. Any more than one ticket is a waste of money. Put it this way. Let's say the odds are fourteen million to one against you winning the lottery. That's to say you have one chance in fourteen million of winning the lottery. This means that there are 13,999,999 chances of you NOT winning the lottery.

OK, so if you buy TWO tickets, what does this do to your chances? Yup, that's right –

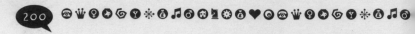

there are now 'only' 13,999,998 chances of you not winning the lottery.

It's not worth the extra outlay.

WELL, IT'S OBVIOUS, ISN'T IT!

It's better to be approximately right than precisely wrong.

Arms are too short to scratch the middle of the back.

In just two days, tomorrow will be yesterday.

Letting the cat out of the bag is a lot easier than putting it back in.

Sharks will only bite you when you are wet.

The wonderful thing about learning is that nobody can take it away from you.

Today is the last day of your life, so far.

An eye for an eye makes the whole world blind.

For every minute you are angry you lose sixty seconds of happiness.

The word *listen* contains the same letters as the word *silent*.

How long a minute is depends on what side of the bathroom door you're on.

Democracy must be something more than two wolves and a sheep voting on what to have for dinner.

He who laughs last thinks slowest.

It's nice to be important, but it's important to be nice.

A pig in silk clothing is still a pig.

A smile is a curve that sets everything straight.

Everybody is ignorant – only on different subjects.

The quickest way to double your money is to fold it over and put it back in your pocket.

If something sounds too good to be true, then it probably is.

Anything free is worth what you pay for it.

Everyone is beautiful if you squint a bit (though sometimes you have to squint quite a lot).

You live and learn, or you don't live long.

The more alternatives, the more difficult the choice.

If everyone supports the underdog, he ceases to be the underdog.

It is the dull person who is always sure, and the sure person who is always dull.

One nice thing about egotists: they don't talk about other people.

If a plan is stupid, and it works, it isn't stupid.

TRUTHS FOR PESSIMISTS

The light at the end of the tunnel is almost certainly a NO EXIT sign.

After all is said and done, more is said than done.

Success always occurs in private, and failure in full view.

If during a month only three enjoyable social activities take place, they will all happen on the same day.

If work were good for you, the rich would leave none for the poor.

Nothing is so good as it seems beforehand.

We are born naked, wet and hungry. Then things get worse.

When things are going easy, it's a sign that you are going downhill.

If you really want to make an enemy, do someone a favour.

No one's listening – until you make a mistake.

For every action there is an equal and opposite criticism.

No amount of planning will ever replace dumb luck.

When things are going easy, it's a sign that you are going downhill.

To the optimist, the glass is half full. To the pessimist, the glass is half empty.

TRUTHS FOR OPTIMISTS

The difference between an optimist and a pessimist? The optimist invents the aeroplane, the pessimist invents the parachute.

Whatever doesn't kill you makes you stronger.

Life isn't tied with a bow, but it's still a gift.

If there were no clouds, we wouldn't enjoy the sun.

If you don't care where you are, then you're not lost.

An optimist is someone who hasn't heard the bad news.

NOW, HOW TRUE IS THAT!

You only live once – but if you work it right, once is enough.

Advice is what we ask for when we already know the answer but wish we didn't.

Freedom of speech is wonderful – right up there with the freedom not to listen.

Beauty without grace is the hook without bait.

Every snowflake in an avalanche pleads not guilty.

If you owe the bank £100, that's your problem. If you owe the bank £100 million, that's the bank's problem.

Everything should be made as simple as possible, but not one bit simpler.

The happiest people don't necessarily have the best of everything (they almost certainly don't); they just make the most of

everything that comes their way.

The best things in life aren't things.

A conclusion is simply the place where you got tired of thinking.

Failure is not falling down, it is not getting up again.

The shepherd has to persuade the sheep that his interests and their interests are the same.

Good judgement comes from experience, and experience comes from bad judgement.

Vision without action is a daydream; action without vision is a nightmare.

Fools are always certain of themselves; wiser people are always full of doubts.

You never find something you've lost until you replace it.

However good or bad a situation is, it will change.

You can keep throwing up long after you think you're finished.

Motivation comes in short bursts. Act while it's hot.

Everything is always OK in the end; if it's not OK, then it's not the end.

The people who tell you 'There's a time for work and a time for play' never seem to find the time for play.

A truly happy person is one who can enjoy the scenery on a detour.

No matter what happens, somebody will find a way to take it too seriously.

The best way to be happy is to make other people happy.

What other people do to you is not your fault; what you allow them to do to you is.

Everyone has a photographic memory. It's just that some people don't have film.

It takes years to build up trust, and only seconds to destroy it.

Life is an open door. It can be closed at any time, so don't complain about the draught.

It's better to arrive ten minutes late in this

life than ten years early in the next.

Bills travel through the post at twice the speed of cheques.

Learning from your own mistakes is clever; learning from the mistakes of others is wise.

The eyes believe themselves; the ears believe other people.

War does not determine who is right – only who is left.

Everything has its beauty, but not everyone sees it.

The best knowledge is to know yourself.

Success usually comes to those who are too busy to be looking for it.

Speak when you are angry – and you will make the best speech you'll ever regret.

The difference between pretty and beautiful is that pretty is temporary but beautiful is for ever.

TRUTHS ABOUT HAPPINESS

Happiness is when what you think, what you say, and what you do are in harmony.

Happiness is always a by-product.

Happiness is even sweeter when you make others believe they are the cause of it.

Happiness isn't something you experience; it's something you remember.

Happiness is largely up to you: most people are about as happy as they make up their minds to be.

Happiness isn't having what you want; it's wanting what you have.

Happiness is a highway, not a destination. *In other words, it is better to travel hopefully than it is to arrive (doesn't apply to car journeys with the family).*

TRUTHS ABOUT SUCCESS

Nothing changes your opinion of a friend so surely as success – yours or theirs.
There are friends who are there for you when things go badly and friends who are there for you when things go well. If it's the same friend for both, then he or she is undoubtedly your best friend. But bear in mind the same is almost certainly also true when it comes to YOU in your role as a friend.

Success isn't permanent, and failure isn't fatal.

A minute's success pays the failure of years.

Success is the ability to go from one failure to another with no loss of enthusiasm.

Aim for success, not perfection.
Perfection is almost impossible to achieve, and those who strive for it usually fail. Think of it like an exam: if 50 per cent is a

pass and 70 per cent is a top grade, then success is anywhere between those two figures (depending upon your aptitude for that exam). So to strive to get 100 per cent is not only unnecessary; it might actually lead to you failing altogether if the strain of so much effort gets to you.

Success is getting what you want. Happiness is liking what you get.

Nothing succeeds like success.

Consider also the following statement: Nothing succeeds like the appearance of success.

This is very true. Years ago, I was writing questions for a phenomenally successful game called Trivial Pursuit. In truth, I didn't earn much money from it but, more important, people thought I did. So when I did work for those people, they treated me as a successful person and paid me more than they would have done if they'd thought I was unsuccessful. It might not be fair – in fact, it almost certainly isn't – to pay wealthy people more than poor people, but it's the way of the world and I merely invite you to bear it in mind (albeit for the future).

TRUTHS ABOUT FOOLS

Fools rush in where fools have been before.

Fools will ask more questions in an hour than a wise person can answer in several years.

The wise profit more from fools than fools from the wise.

When arguing with a fool, make sure they're not doing the same.

OK. I'll meet you half-way. I'll admit I'm wrong if you admit I'm right.

Sometimes a majority only means that all the fools are on the same side.

Nothing is more valuable than time. That's why fools waste it.

Fool me once, shame on you. Fool me twice, shame on me.

Fools are known by their words; the wise by their actions.

Fools know everything and understand nothing.

Fools talk because they have to say something; the wise talk because they have something to say.

A fool and his money are soon parted.
Though I also like the idea that a fool and his money are soon partying . . .

NB. Nothing is foolproof to a truly ambitious fool.

PROVERBS WITH MORE THAN JUST A HINT OF TRUTH TO THEM

Advice is least heeded when most needed.
Which is why – as you'll see elsewhere in this book – to give advice is bad; to give good advice is fatal.

After the game, the king and the pawn go into the same box.
Ultimately, we all have to learn to live with one another.

I enjoyed that game, I felt really moved!

Good fences make good neighbours.
*Obviously it's desirable and important to
get on with your neighbours, and one way
to achieve that is to make sure there are
clear boundaries between you that neither*

side can dispute and which help to protect both sides from the other's worst habits. Applies, of course, to countries and their borders as much as it does to householders.

No one can make you feel inferior without your consent.
It really does take two, so don't help someone who's trying to make you feel small.

Whoever gossips *to* you will gossip *about* you.
So, as much as you enjoy gossip, beware gossips.

Things turn out best for those who make the best of the way things turn out.
In other words, learning to accept – and deal – with situations which are maybe not to your choosing will result in happiness.

How we spend our days, of course, is how we spend our lives.
Ultimately, we are what we do regularly.

What we do willingly is easy.
If you have to do something, do it graciously . . . you'll enjoy it more, and the person you're helping will appreciate it too.

When children stand quiet, they have done some harm.

Hmm . . . it is a bit of a dead giveaway.

Who has never tasted bitter knows not what is sweet.

It's all about living a full, varied life. If all you do is have fun, eventually the fun becomes boring. We need the contrast.

All doors open to courtesy.

Even if they didn't, it would still be the right way to behave.

An unfortunate man would be drowned in a teacup.

This is neither literally – nor metaphorically – true, and yet this proverb does illustrate the fact that when someone is undergoing a period of really bad fortune, almost anything will defeat them.

You are the architect of your own fortunes – and misfortunes.

Not always, but much of the time, it really is up to you to decide just how happy or unhappy you want to be. And even when you're not in control of events, it is still your choice how you react to them.

The darkest hour is just before the dawn.
*When you're lying in bed, worrying about
something you have to do that day, the
very worst time is just before you're due to
get up: you take on board all the worries,
all the awful things that you know are going
to happen. But if you can just shut out the
demons till you get up and are busy getting
ready for the day, those worries will, I
promise, recede and even vanish altogether.
The worrying is almost always worse than
the thing we're worrying about. By the
same token, never try to solve serious
matters in the middle of the night.*

Virtue is its own reward.
*It's important to do the right thing –
irrespective of whether there's a reward
or not. The knowledge that you've done
the right thing really is a true reward.
Though that's not to say that you wouldn't
feel a teensy bit cheated if you handed a
full wallet in to the police station and the
owner didn't give you a penny . . .*

When the well's dry, we know the worth of water.
We only truly value things/people when they're no longer around.

Health is not valued till sickness comes.
*Just like not knowing the value of water till
the well is dry . . .*

What can't be cured must be endured.
*Old proverb that I use whenever I'm in
a situation where I have no control. Let's
say I'm in a traffic jam on a motorway and
I'm short of time. I could shout, scream
and swear . . . or I could merely shrug my
shoulders and say, 'What can't be cured,
must be endured.' Usually, I do both.*

A little knowledge is a dangerous thing.
*Well, maybe not dangerous, but it can be
misleading when you know a tiny bit about
a subject and start to make big assumptions
based on that knowledge. Journalists –
and I am one – are frequently likely to be
caught out by this as we become instant
'experts' on lots of subjects and only realize
how little we know when real experts start
asking us questions.*

A gentle stream can split a mountain, given enough time.
A proverb that illustrates the importance of persistence . . . and patience.

It's better to give a rock out of love than a diamond out of duty.
All gifts should be given with the right motivation – i.e. love, affection, respect. However, it is also true to say that there are people who would rather receive a diamond than a rock and, er, take a chance on the donor's motives . . .

Health is the primary duty of life.
Look after yourself. You only have one body, so don't wreck it with junk food or – worse – cigarettes.

Silence is sometimes the best answer.
Indeed, sometimes the cleverest things are said in silence.

he test of courage comes when we are in the minority. The test of tolerance comes when we are in the majority.

You need to have the courage of your convictions – especially when others are howling you down. As for tolerance, it is almost always something that the majority extends to the minority. The fact that you don't like something is what makes it so important to tolerate it (unless it's a bad thing): that's why it's called tolerance and not approval.

Who breaks, pays.

Well, SOMEONE has to . . . and it might as well be the person who did it.

People who live in glass houses shouldn't throw stones.

If you're vulnerable in an area of your life, then you're silly to tease other people about their vulnerability in that area (or indeed in ANY other area). Unless you can take it as easily as you dish it out.

Excellence is not a singular act but a habit.
*It's no good just doing well occasionally:
you have to keep on doing well. Ultimately,
there's a case for saying that you are what
you do repeatedly.*

Worry makes for a hard pillow.
*An old proverb illustrating the great truth
that NOTHING is worth losing sleep over.*

ᴥmooth seas don't make skilful sailors.
You only REALLY learn to sail properly when you've tackled tough weather. In other words, it's only by testing ourselves that we hone our strengths.

That which is bitter to endure may be sweet to remember.
It's an old proverb – which is why it's couched in such old language – but it happens to be true: a bit of pain in the present might lead to a lot of pleasure in the future (especially when it comes to exams!).

No winter lasts for ever; no spring skips its turn.
Whatever happens, the world marches on – impervious to you and your concerns.

By learning you will teach; by teaching you will learn.
You've heard of 'a vicious circle'? Well, this is the opposite – what you might call a virtuous circle. Having learned things, you can pass them on; as you pass things

on, you learn more things. The two don't have to happen at the same time, but they might!

He who is afraid to ask is ashamed of learning.
There's another saying that fits in really well here: He who asks is a fool for five minutes, but he who does not ask remains a fool for ever.

To give advice is bad; to give good advice is fatal.
Particularly when that 'good advice' hasn't been asked for.

It is ill manners to silence the fool, and cruelty to let him go on.
What can you do!

Here are some more examples of idiotic, fatal behaviour from those Darwin Awards...

Attempting to play Russian roulette with a semi-automatic pistol that automatically reloads the next round into the chamber.

Using a lighter to illuminate a fuel tank to make sure it contains nothing flammable.

Crashing through a window and falling to your death while trying to demonstrate that the window is unbreakable.

Juggling active hand grenades.

Jumping out of a plane to film skydivers without wearing a parachute.

Trying to get enough light to look down the barrel of a loaded muzzleloader gun using a cigarette lighter.

Attempting Russian roulette with an unexploded landmine.

And here are some more unbelievably moronic tales for you to ponder over

A pack of thieves attempted to steal scrap metal from an abandoned factory in the Czech Republic. Unfortunately for them, they selected the steel girders that supported the factory roof. When the roof supports were dismantled, the roof fell in, fatally crushing two thieves and injuring three others.

An Iraqi terrorist didn't put enough stamps on a letter bomb and it came back marked RETURN TO SENDER. He opened the package and was blown up.

Two German animal rights activists protesting against cruelty to pigs released 2,000 of them and were promptly trampled to death.

An American man tried stealing the office safe, but was crushed to death when it fell on top of him while he was taking it down the stairs. To make matters worse, the 250-kg safe was empty.

A keen American hunter was having a row with his girlfriend and used the butt of his shotgun to bash in her windscreen. Unfortunately, his loaded gun accidentally discharged into his stomach and killed him.

A German man attempting to impress his wife with his unbelievable strength climbed over the balcony of their seventh-floor flat, clung to the outside of the parapet, and began a set of pull-ups. After a few of these, he was exhausted and couldn't pull himself back onto the balcony. He fell seven floors to his death, impaling himself on a thornbush.

Matthew was sliding down a Mammoth Mountain ski run on a yellow foam pad when he crashed into a lift tower and died.

He would have been fine, but the yellow foam designed to protect skiers had been stolen . . . by Matthew for his makeshift sledge.

An American man shot himself while explaining gun safety to his wife. He placed a .45-calibre pistol he thought was unloaded under his chin and pulled the trigger.

Two men robbed a store in South Carolina and then fled – but they couldn't flee from their own stupidity, for one of them had disguised himself by painting his face gold. Paint fumes are well-known to be toxic, and the metallic colours are particularly noxious – so, unsurprisingly, the robber began having trouble breathing and died wheezing shortly after the robbery took place.

A young man was kicked out of a Florida bar for fighting. He sneaked back in and leaped off a staircase, aiming a kick at another man, but was killed when he landed on his head.

Two Belgian bankrobbers died in an explosion when they overestimated the quantity of dynamite needed to blow open a cash machine.

Tribal clashes are common in Ghana, and people often resort to witchcraft in the hope of becoming invulnerable to weapons. One group bought a magical potion to render them invincible to bullets. One of the group volunteered to try it out and stood in a clearing while his friends raised their weapons, aimed, fired . . . and killed him.

Two South African muggers were running away from their victims. One of them spotted a fence and leaped over it . . . into the Bengal tiger cage at Bloemfontein Zoo. The tigers had just been fed so they didn't eat him; they simply tore him apart.

An American man named Christopher called 911 and informed the police dispatcher that his neighbour had stabbed him. Deputies arrived quickly, only to find that Christopher had bled to death from stab wounds to his chest. Here's why: suspecting that his neighbour had been helping himself to his (Christopher's) booze, Christopher decided to take revenge on him by stabbing himself and then telling the police that it was the neighbour who'd done it. Christopher died in vain. His deathbed accusation fell on deaf ears, as a witness stated that the neighbour was not in the apartment, and the neighbour offered to take a lie-detector test to demonstrate his innocence.

A Vietnamese lad named Nguyen had been drinking with friends in Hanoi when he pulled out an old detonator he had found. The detonator was about 6cm long and 8cm in diameter, with two wires hanging out of the end. Because it was old and rusty, he said, it couldn't explode. His friends disagreed. To prove his point, Nguyen put the detonator in his mouth

and asked his friend to plug the dangling wires into a 220-volt electrical receptacle. Nguyen was wrong – he died on the way to the hospital.

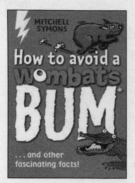

Mitchell Symons
HOW TO AVOID A WOMBAT'S BUM*
And other fascinating facts!

* Don't chase it! Wombats can run up to 25 miles per hour and stop dead in half a stride. They kill their predators this way – the predator runs into the wombat's bum-bone and smashes its face.

Amaze and intrigue your friends and family with more fantastic facts and figures:

- most dinosaurs were no bigger than chickens
- Everton was the first British football club to introduce a stripe down the side of players' shorts
- A snail has about 25,000 teeth
- No piece of paper can be folded in half more than seven times

Just opening this book will have you hooked for hours!

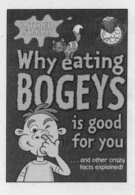

Mitchell Symons
WHY EATING BOGEYS IS GOOD FOR YOU
And other crazy facts explained!

Ever wondered . . .

- Why we have tonsils?
- Is there any cream in cream crackers?
- What's the best way to cure hiccups?
- And if kangaroos keep their babies in their pouches, what happens to all the poo?

Mitchell Symons answers all these wacky questions and plenty more in a wonderfully addictive book that will have you hooked for hours!

(And eating bogeys is good for you . . . but only your own!)

Selected for the Booktrust Booked Up! Initiative in 2008.

Mitchell Symons
HOW MUCH POO DOES AN ELEPHANT DO?*

... and further fascinating facts!

* An elephant produces an eye-wateringly pongy 20 kilograms of dung a day!

Let Mitchell Symons be your guide into the weird and wonderful world of trivia.

- Camels are born without humps
- Walt Disney, creator of Mickey Mouse, was scared of mice
- Only 30% of humans can flare their nostrils
- A group of twelve or more cows is called a flink

Mitchell Symons
WHY DO FARTS SMELL LIKE ROTTEN EGGS?

... and more crazy facts explained!

Ever wondered . . .

- Why we burp?
- What a wotsit is?
- Whether lemmings really jump off cliffs?
- Why vomit always contains carrots?
- And why *do* farts smell like rotten eggs?

No subject is too strange and no trivia too tough for Mitchell Symons, who has the answers to these crazy questions, and many more.

Mitchell Symons

WHY DOES EAR WAX TASTE SO GROSS?*

... and more top trivia!

*stinky ear wax has been hanging around in the ear canal for nearly a month before it is 'pickable'!

Did you know . . .

- **Humans share a third of their DNA with lettuce**

- **Cockroaches fart every fifteen minutes**

- **Giraffes never kneel**

- **The average person spends six months of their life on the loo**

Amaze your mates and fascinate your family with this book packed with jaw-dropping, eyebrow-raising facts!

Mitchell Symons

WHY YOU NEED A PASSPORT WHEN YOU'RE GOING TO PUKE*

. . . and more crazy-
but-true facts!

*Puke is the name of a town in Albania.
Would YOU like to holiday there . . . ?

Did you know . . .

- **Square watermelons are sold in Japan**

- **There is a River Piddle in Dorset**

- **American use enough toilet paper
  daily to wrap around the world
  nine times**

Mitchell Symons goes global – join him
on his fun fact-finding world tour!

Q: Who writes the best books on farts, bogeys and other yucky stuff?

A: Mitchell Symons, of course

Q: What's his website called?

A: Grossbooks.co.uk, what else!

On this site you can:
- Win cool stuff in quizzes and competitions
- Add your own fab facts and publish them online
- Be first to find out about Mitchell's new books before they're published

As Mitchell's mum would say:
'Thank goodness it's not *scratch 'n' sniff*...'

See for yourself at **Grossbooks.co.uk**